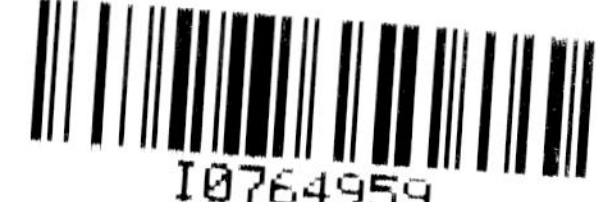

THIS BOOK

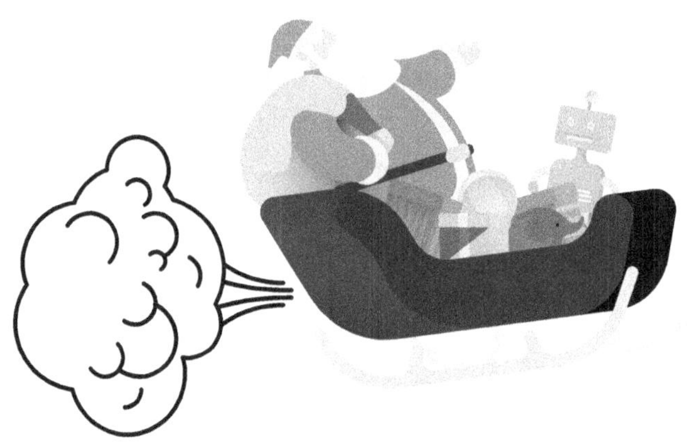

BELONGS
TO

○○○○○○○○○○○○○○○○○○○○○○○○○

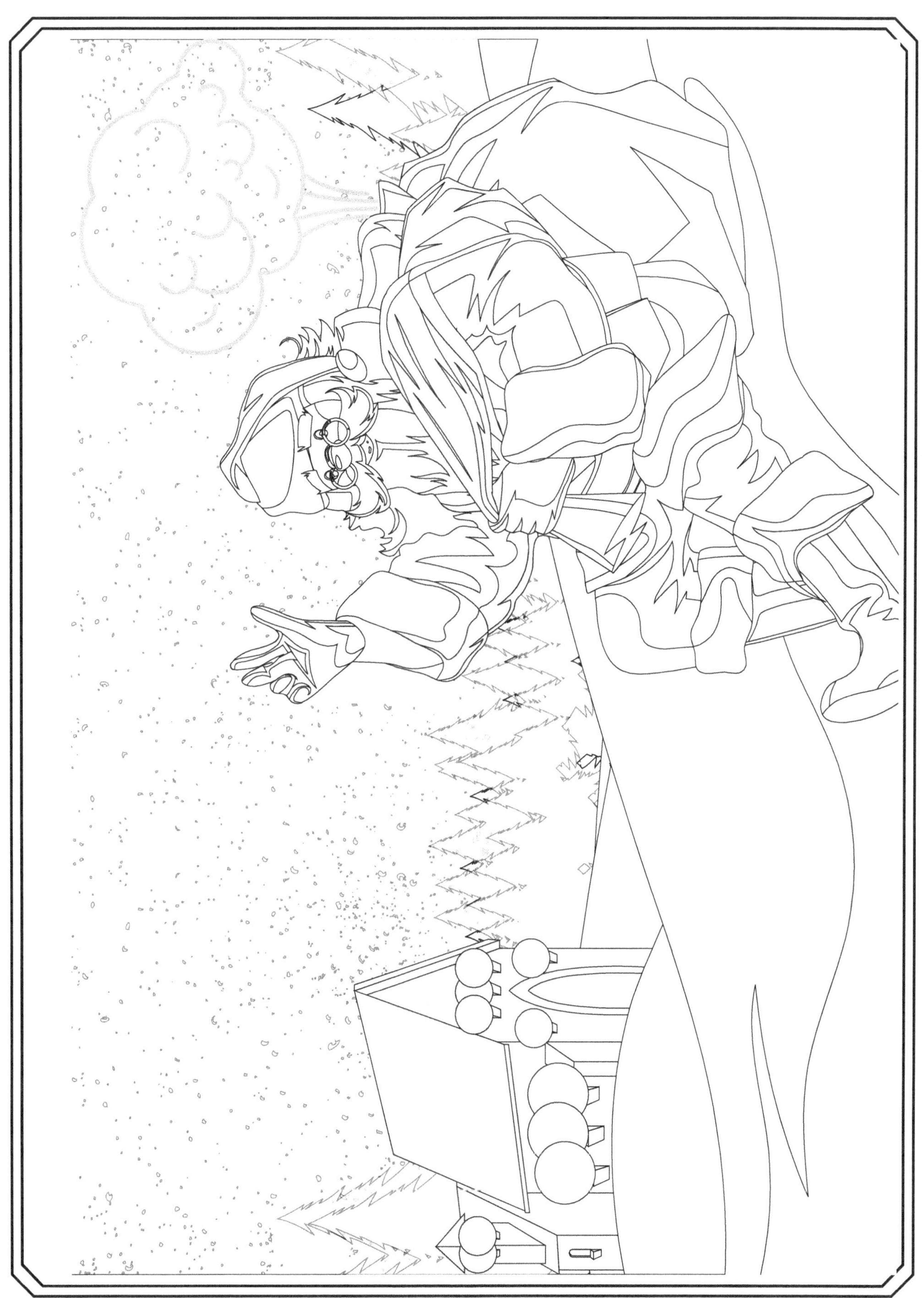

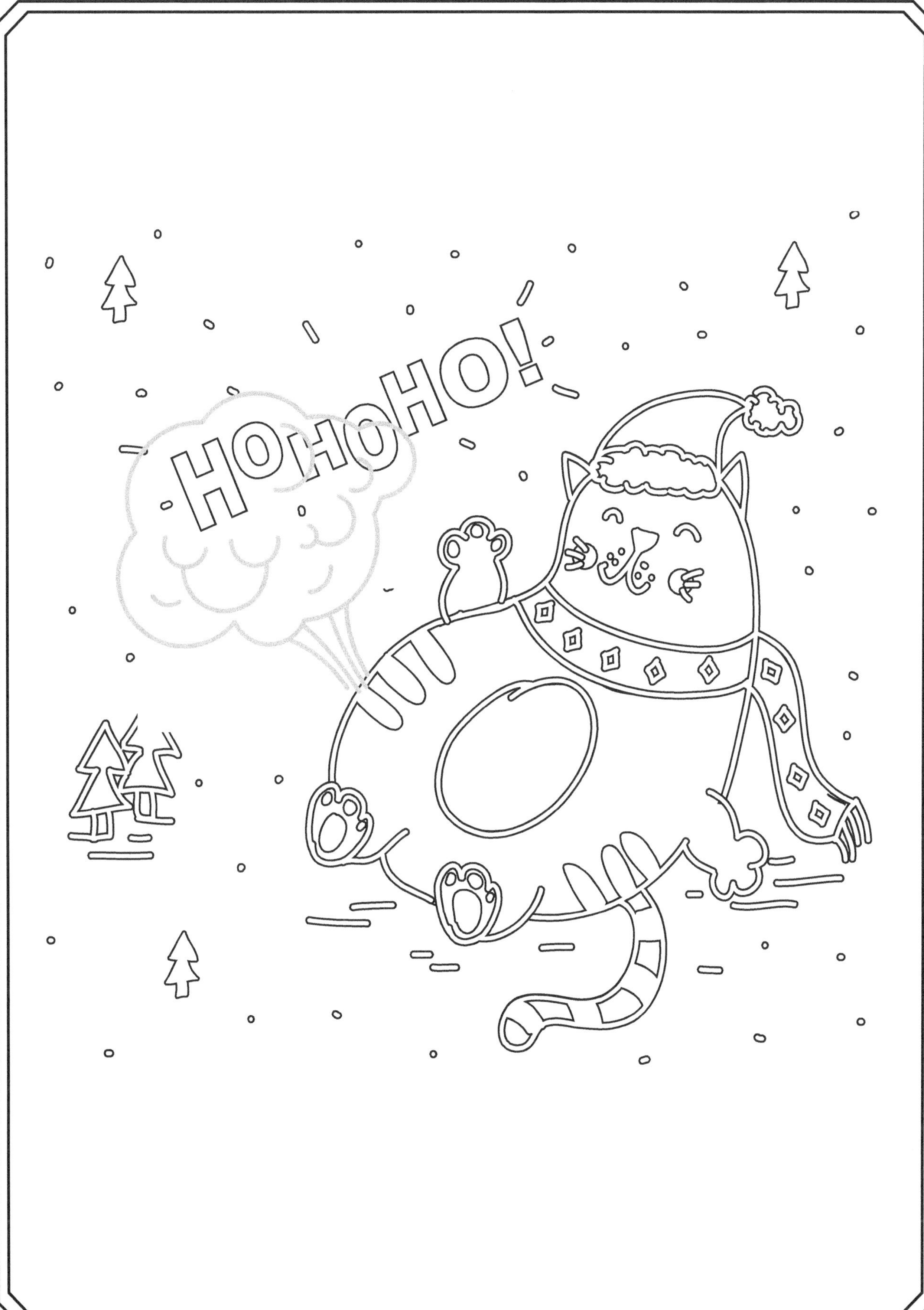

HOHOHO!

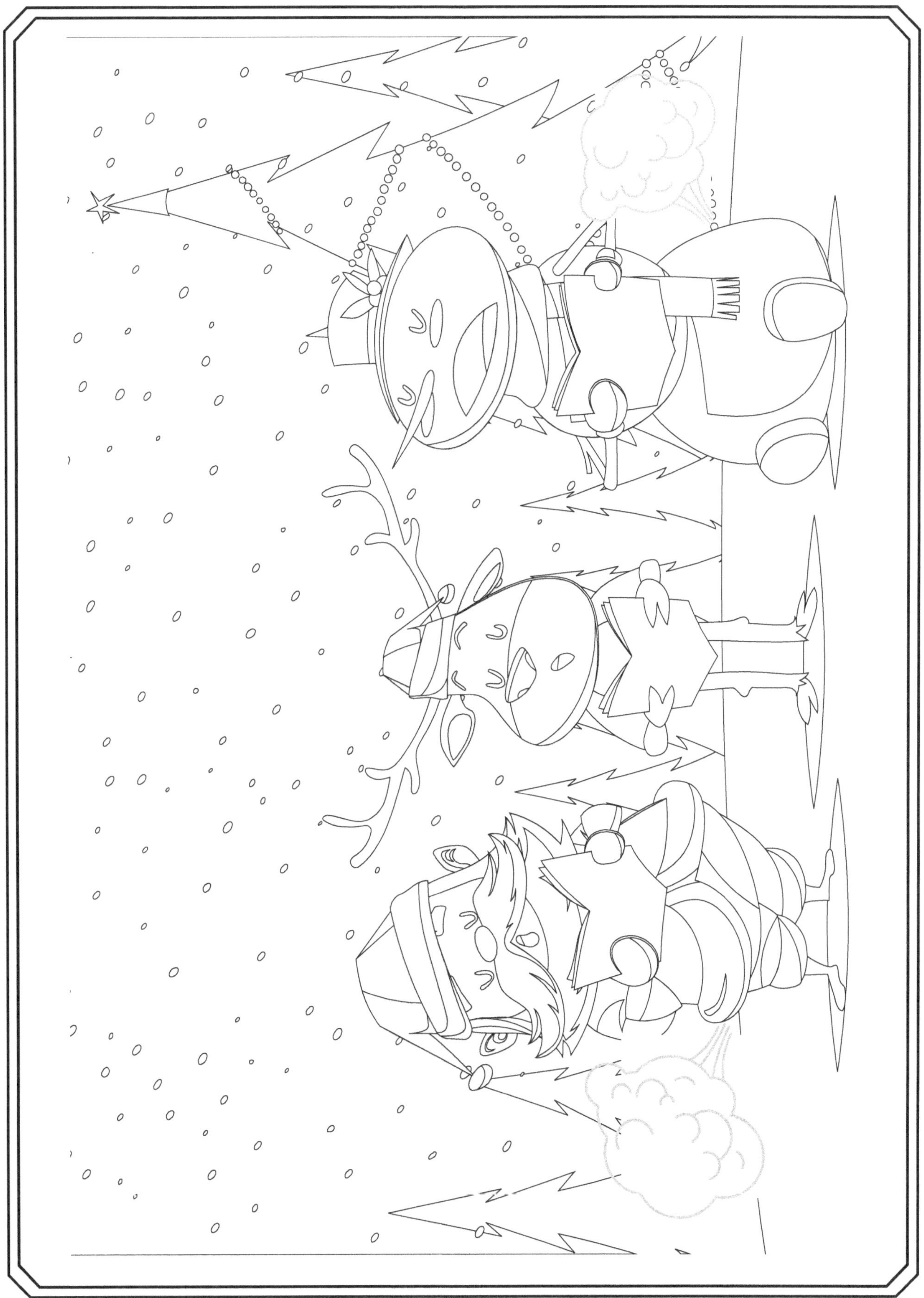

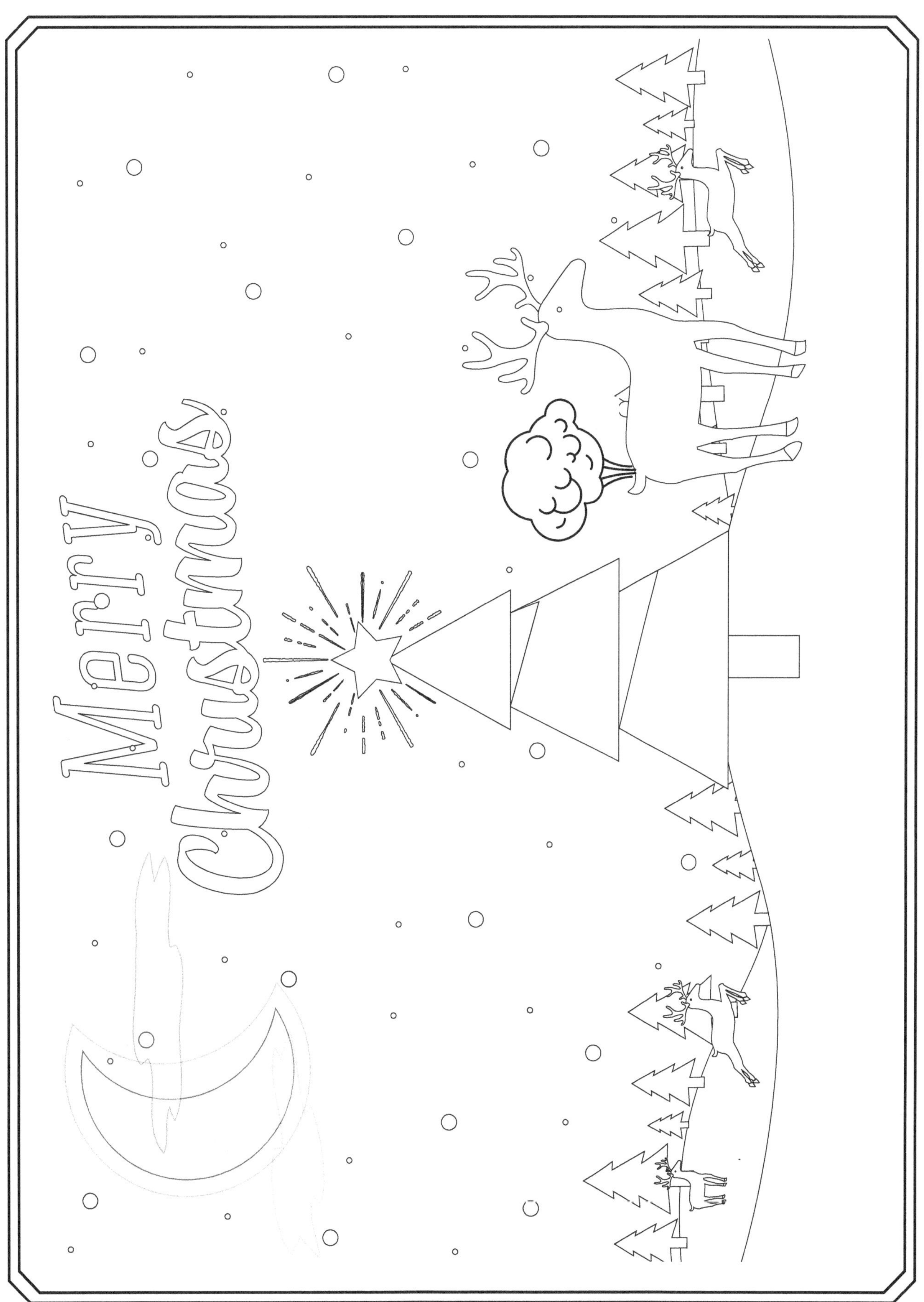
Merry Christmas

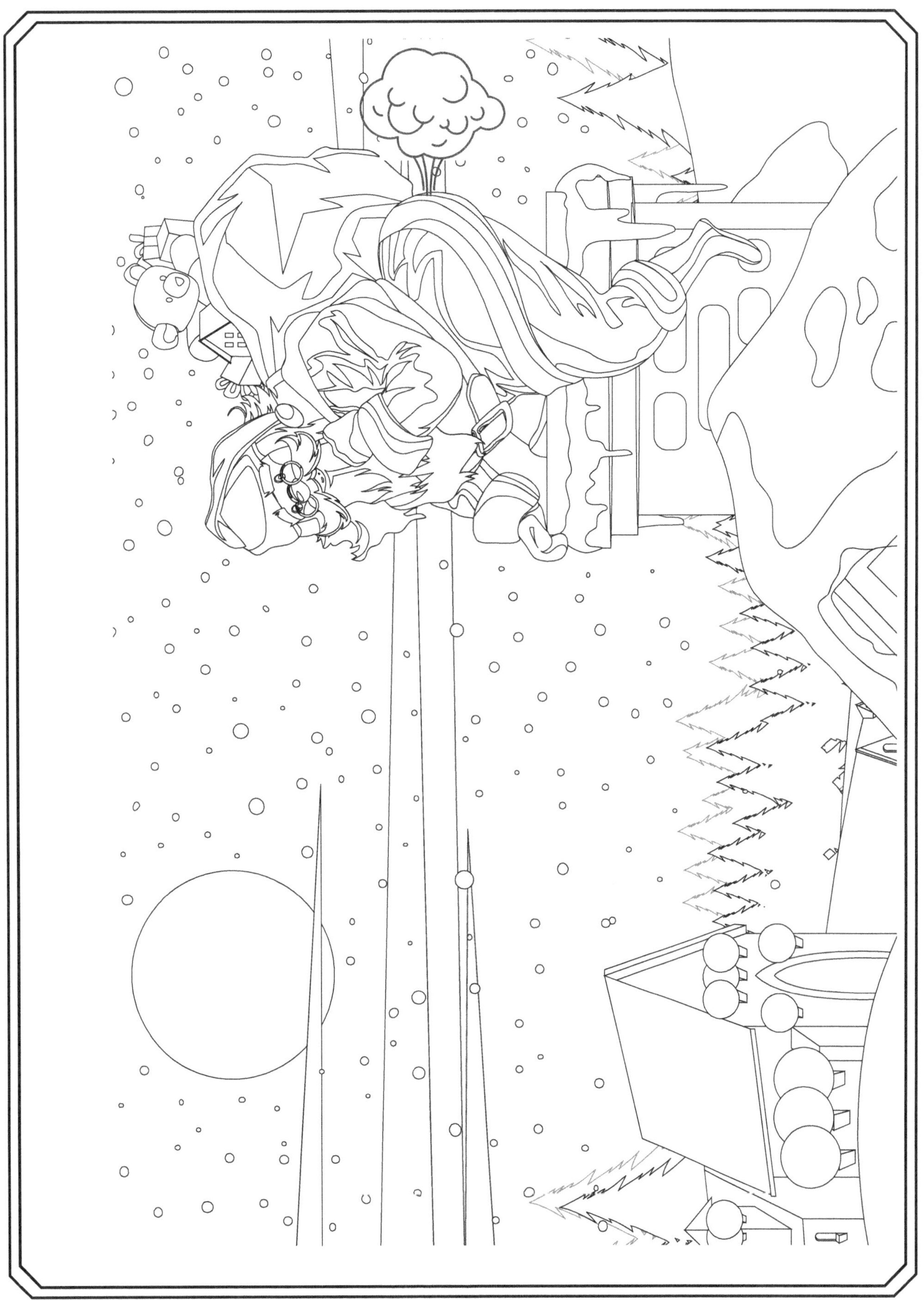

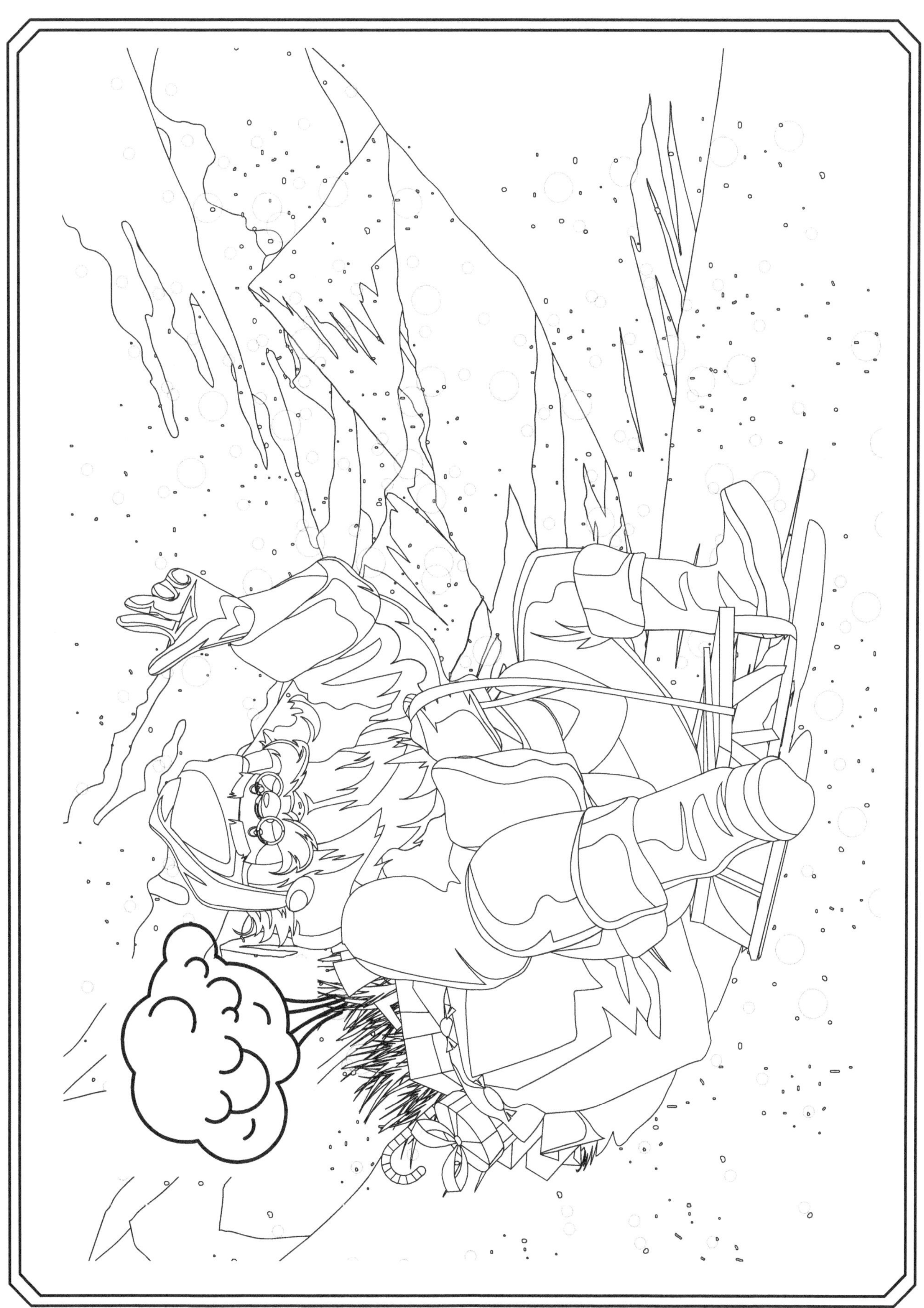

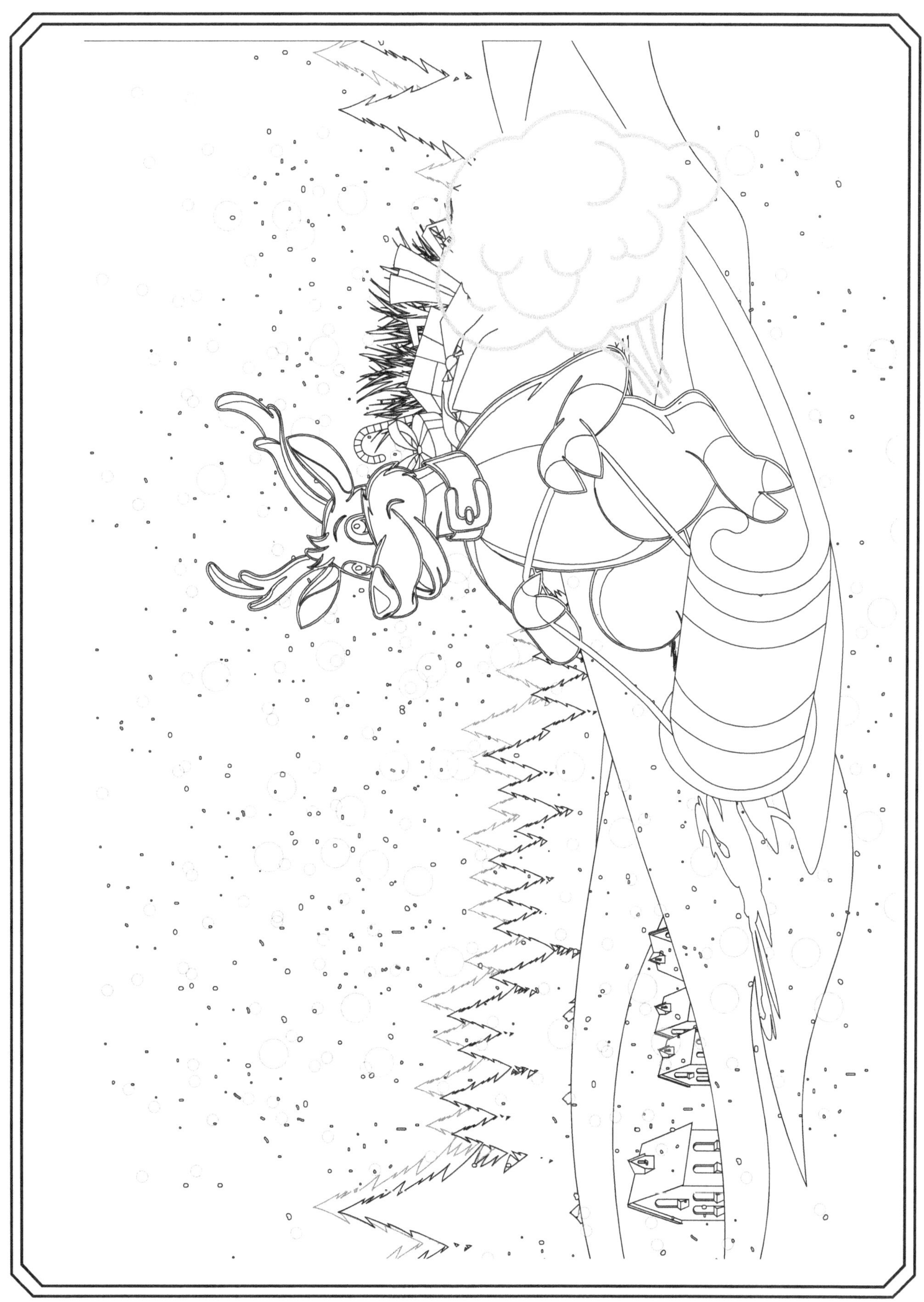

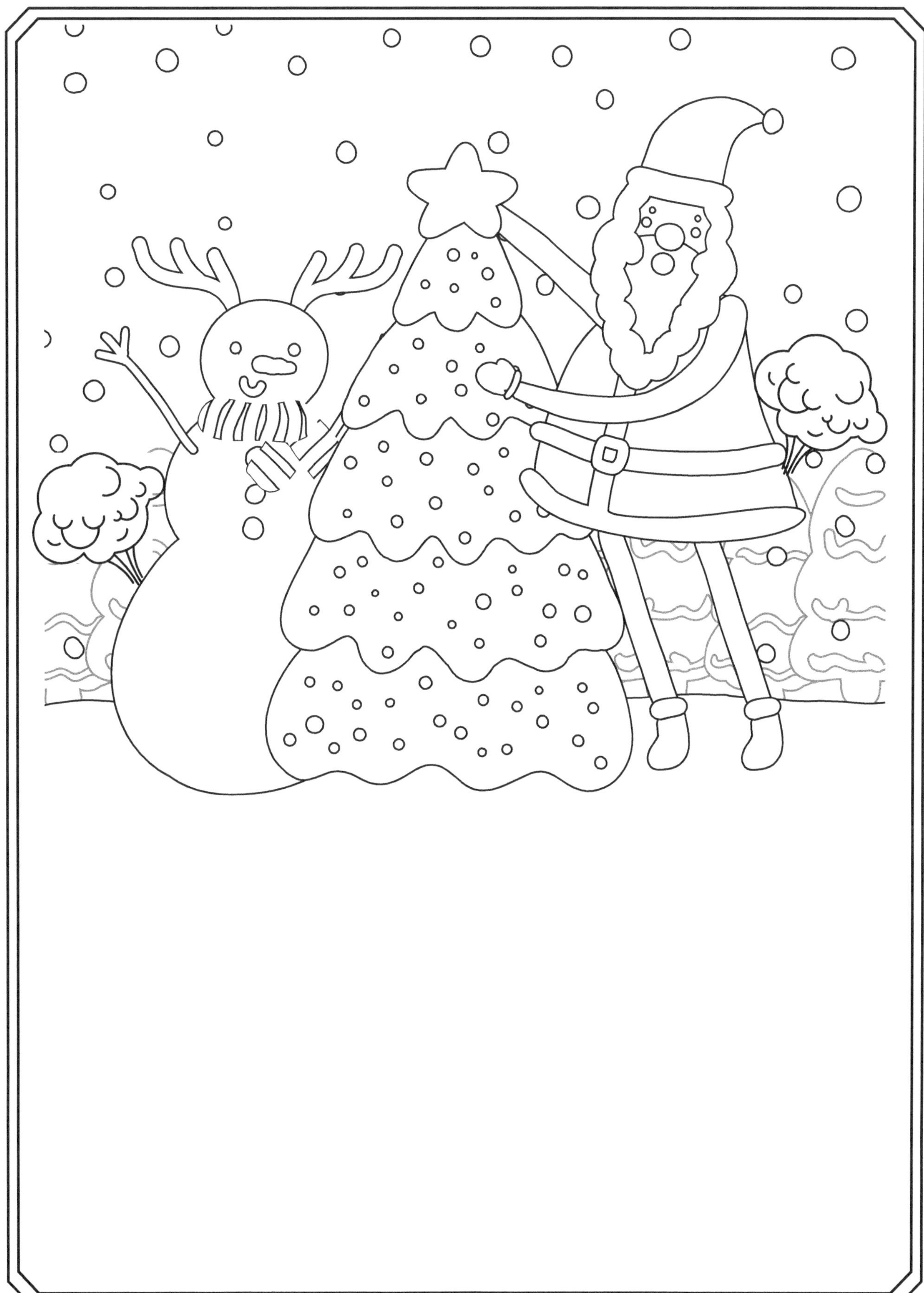

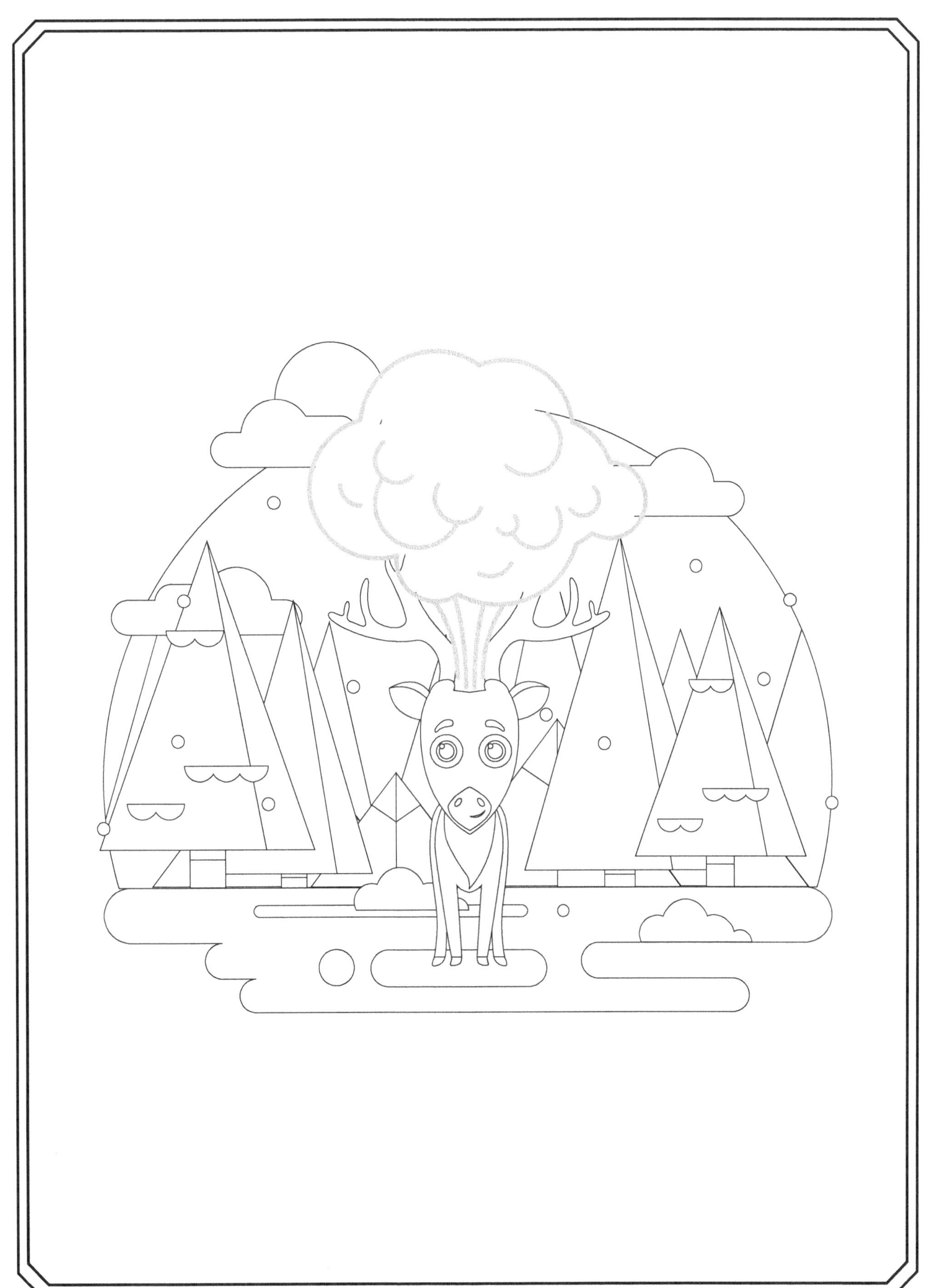

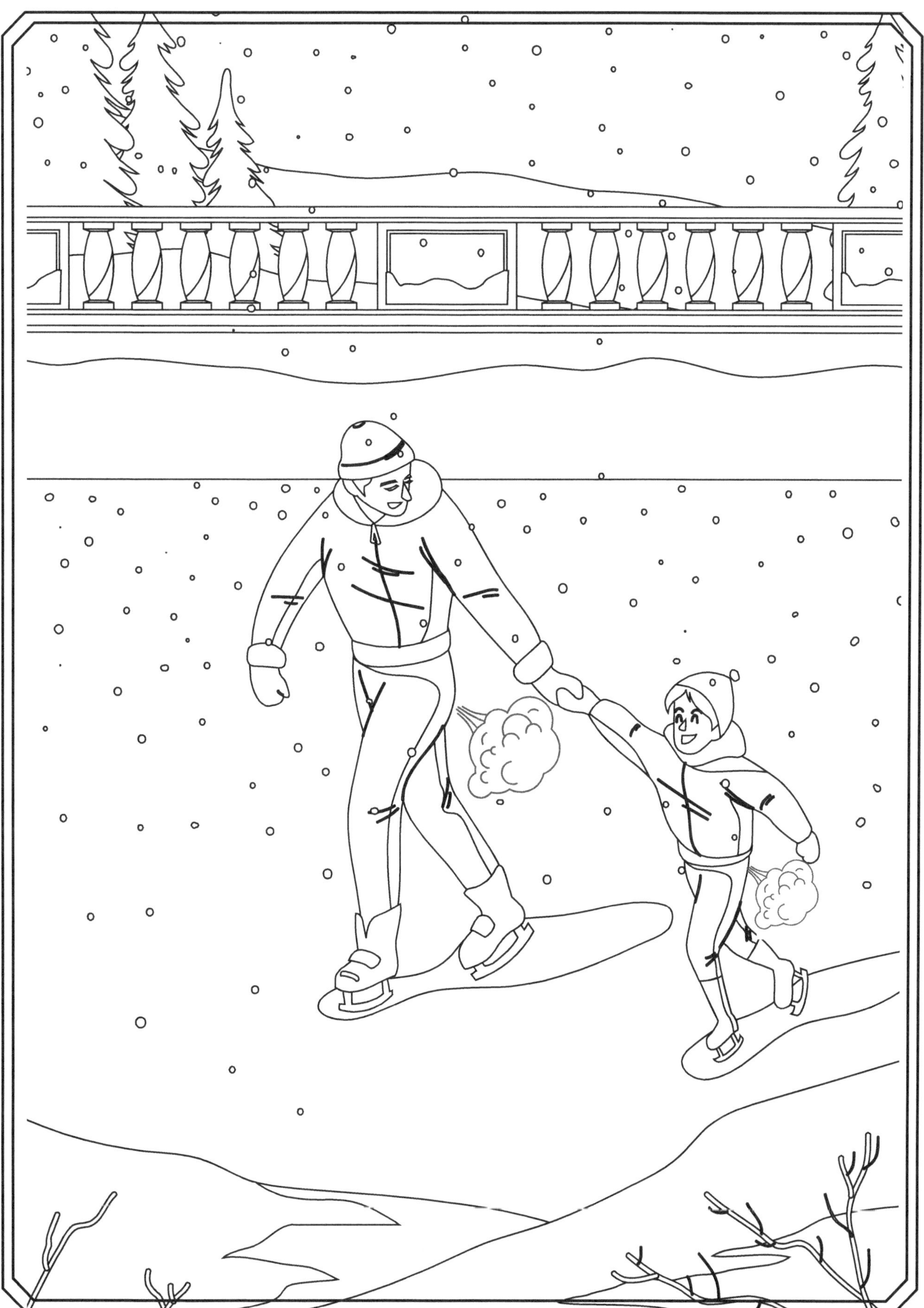

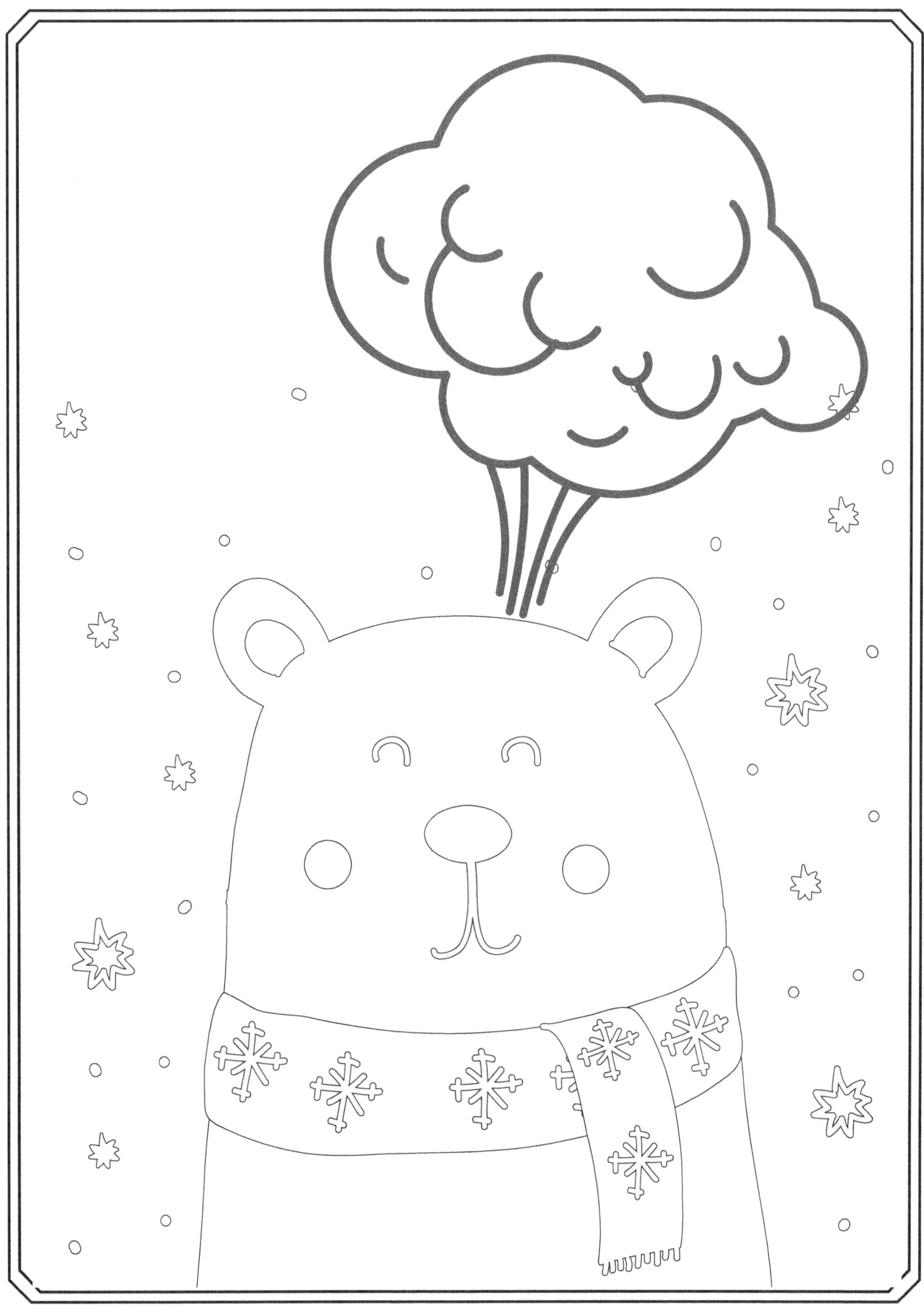

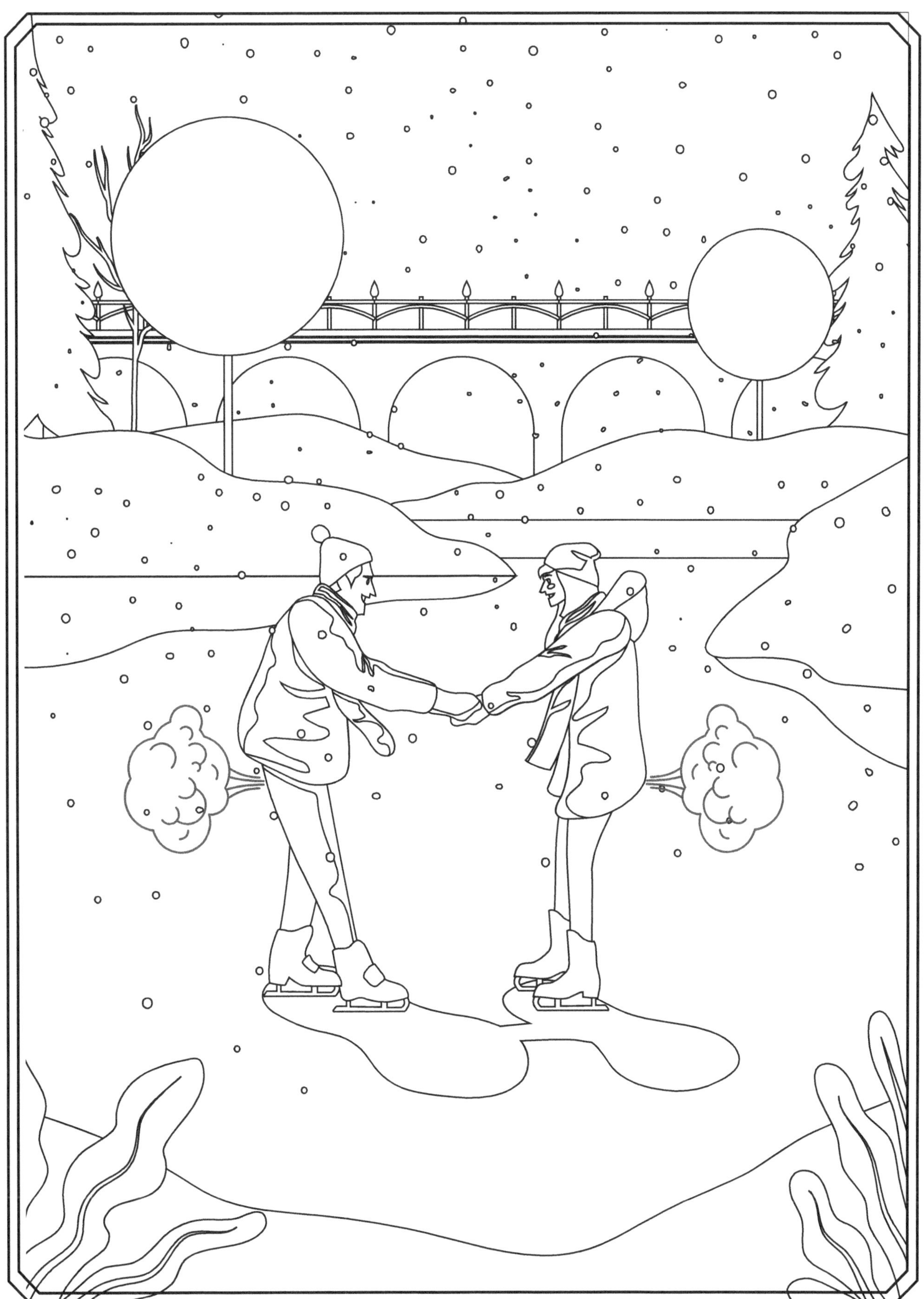

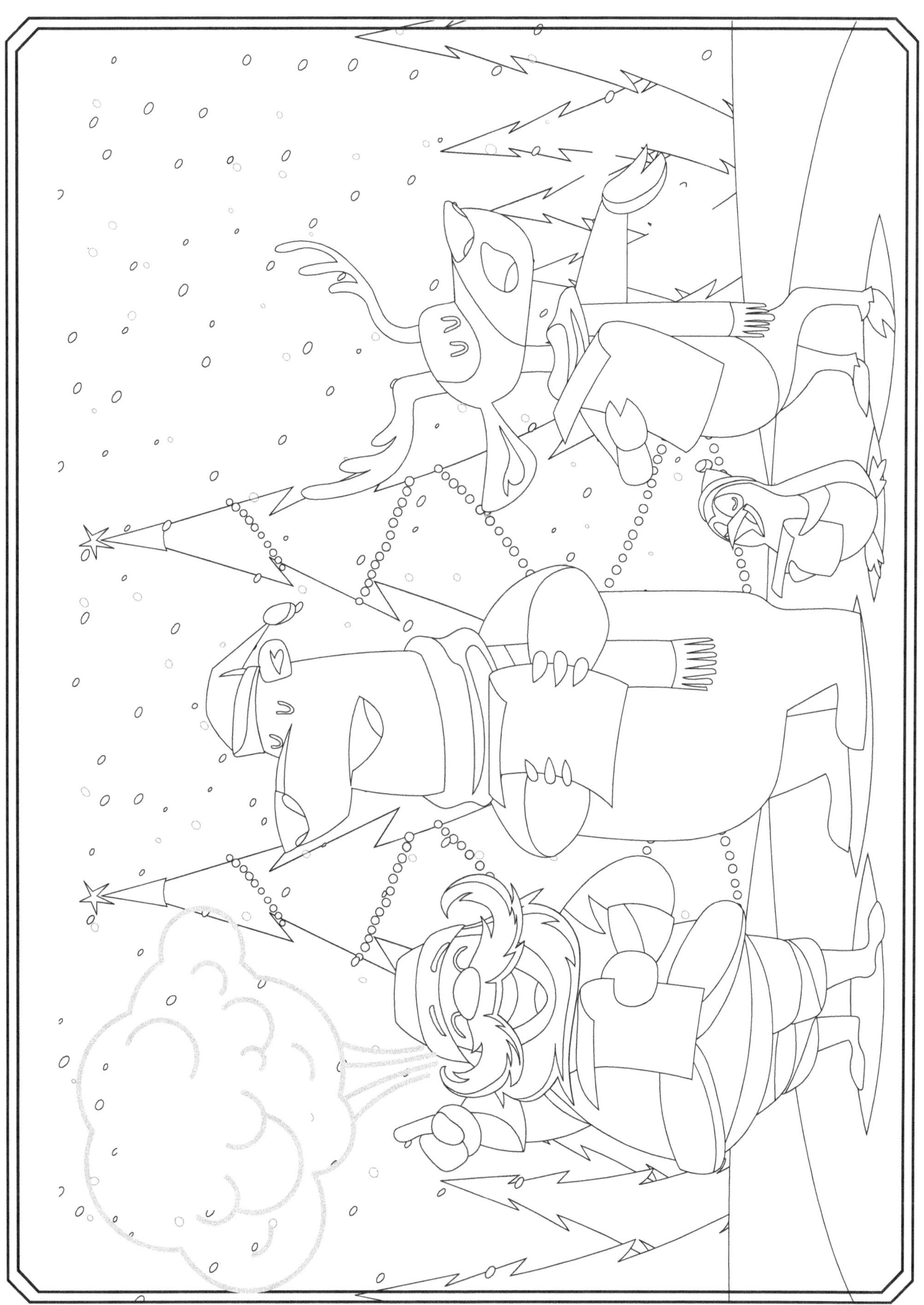

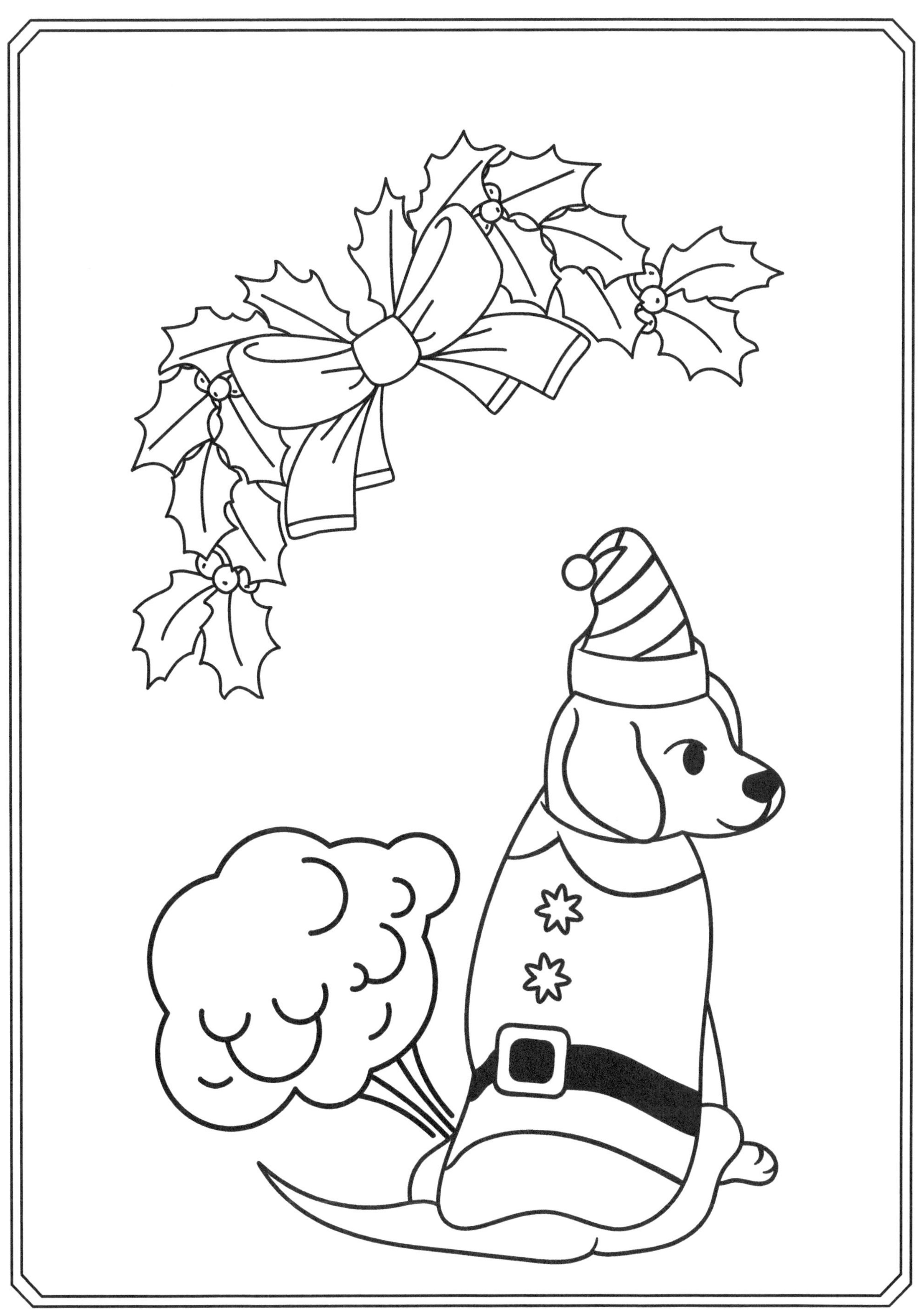

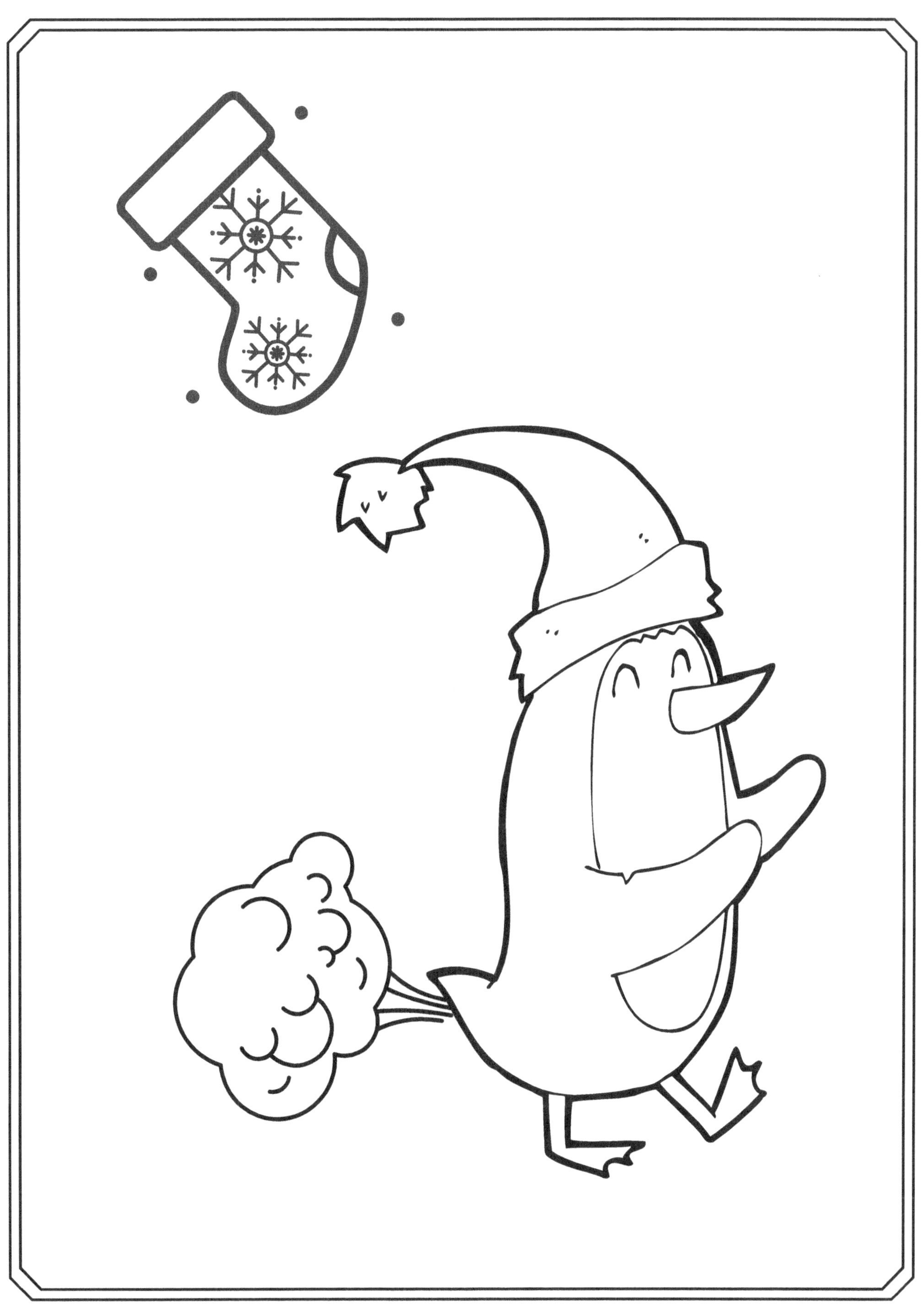